Famous & Fun Pop

11 Appealing Piano Arrangements

Carol Matz

Famous & Fun Pop, Book 1, contains 11 carefully selected popular hits from movies, radio and television. Each piece has been arranged especially for early elementary pianists, yet remains faithful to the sound of the original. All of the arrangements are playable within the first few months of piano instruction, and can be used as a supplement to any method. No eighth notes or dotted-quarter rhythms are used. The optional duet parts for teacher or parent add to the fun. Enjoy your experience with these popular hits!

Supercalifragilisticexpialidocious

(from Walt Disney's "Mary Poppins")

Words and Music by
Richard M. Sherman and Robert B. Sherman
Arranged by Carol Matz

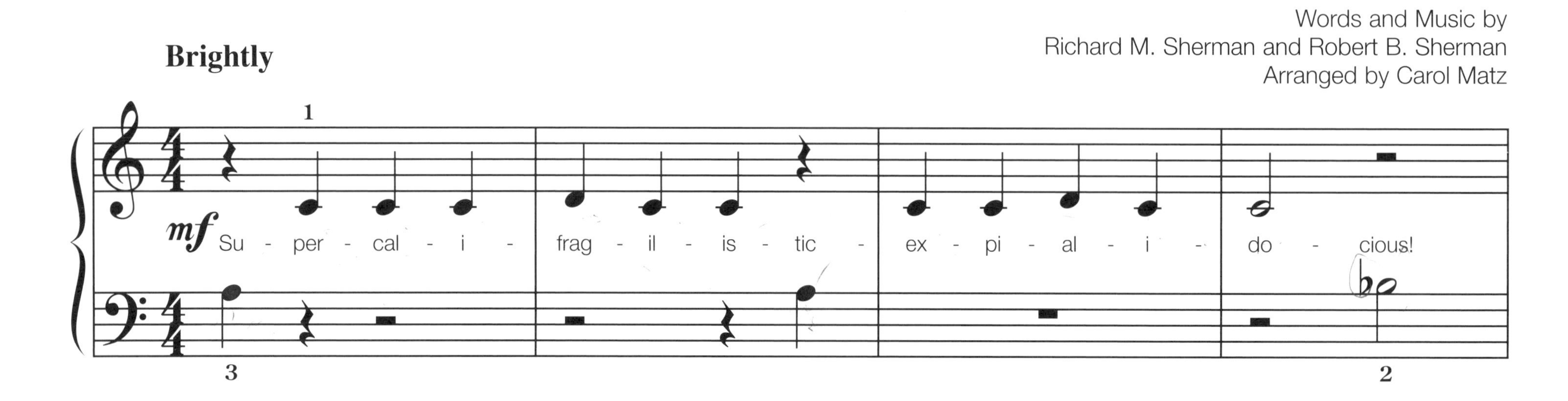

DUET PART (Student plays one octave higher)

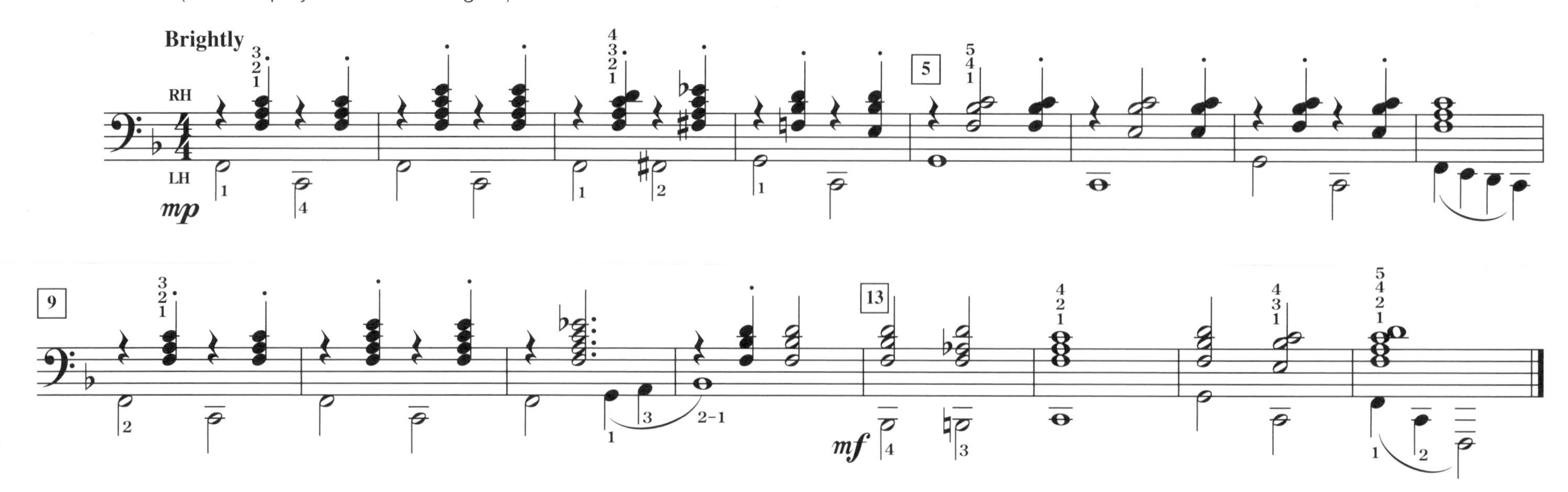

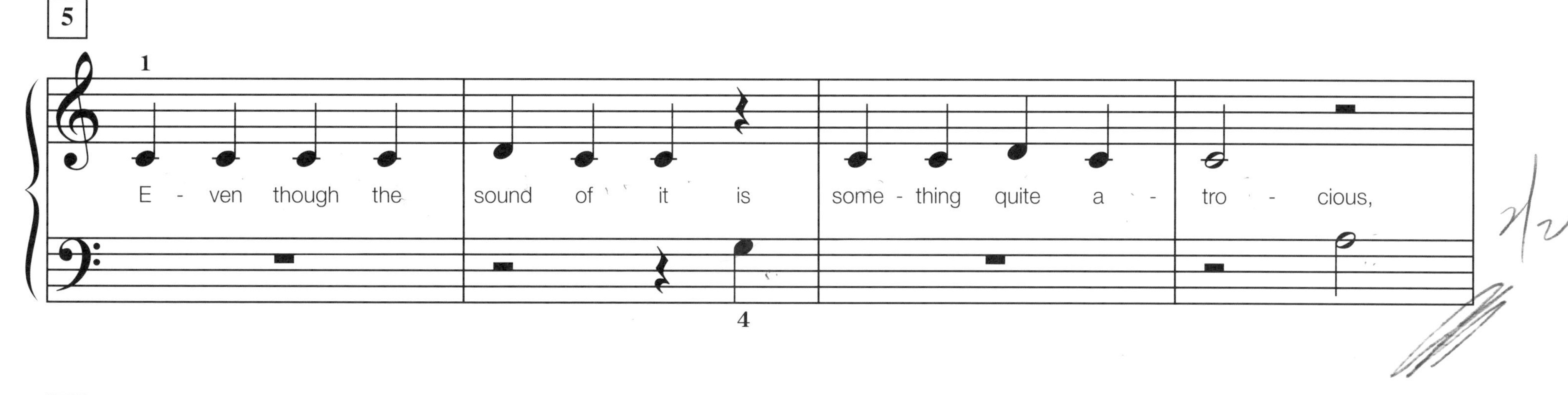
5
1
E - ven though the sound of it is some - thing quite a - tro - cious,
4

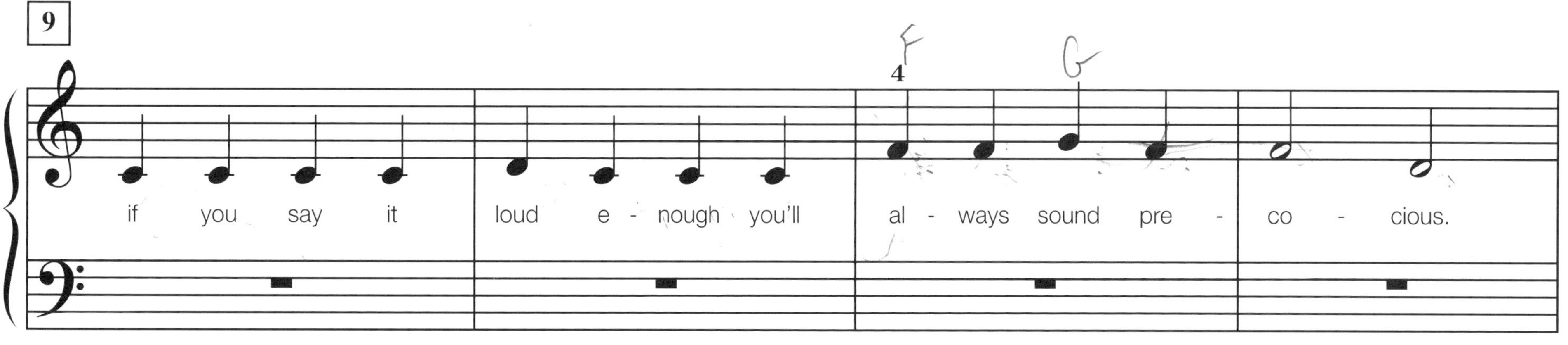
9
4
if you say it loud e - nough you'll al - ways sound pre - co - cious.

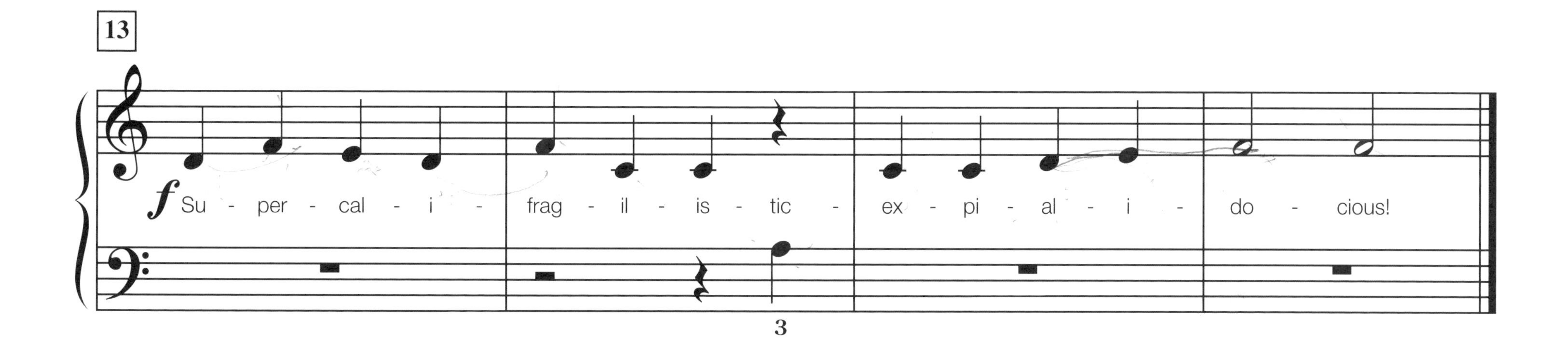
13
f
Su - per - cal - i - frag - il - is - tic - ex - pi - al - i - do - cious!
3

Puff (The Magic Dragon)

Words and Music by
Peter Yarrow and Leonard Lipton
Arranged by Carol Matz

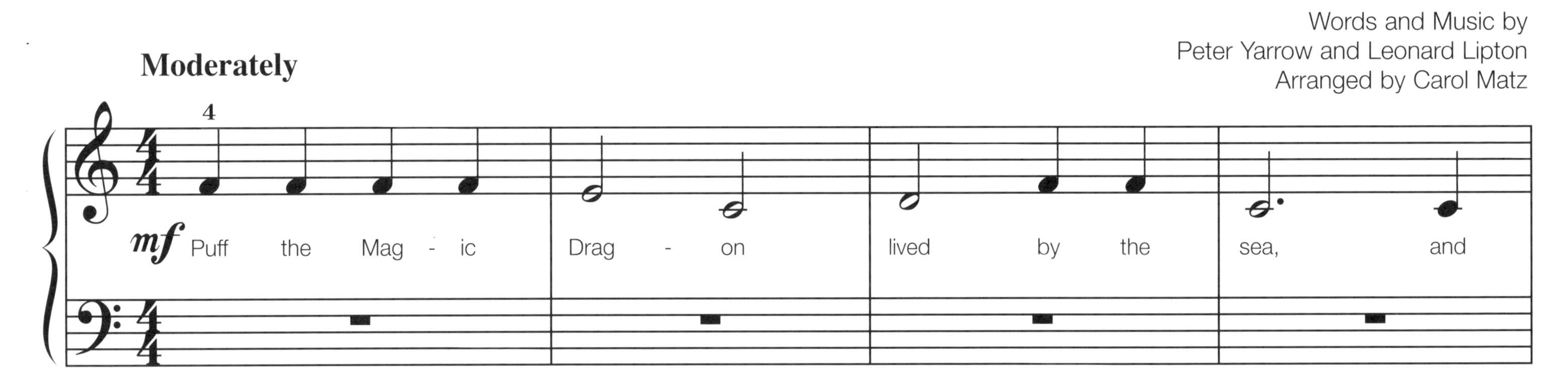

DUET PART (Student plays one octave higher)

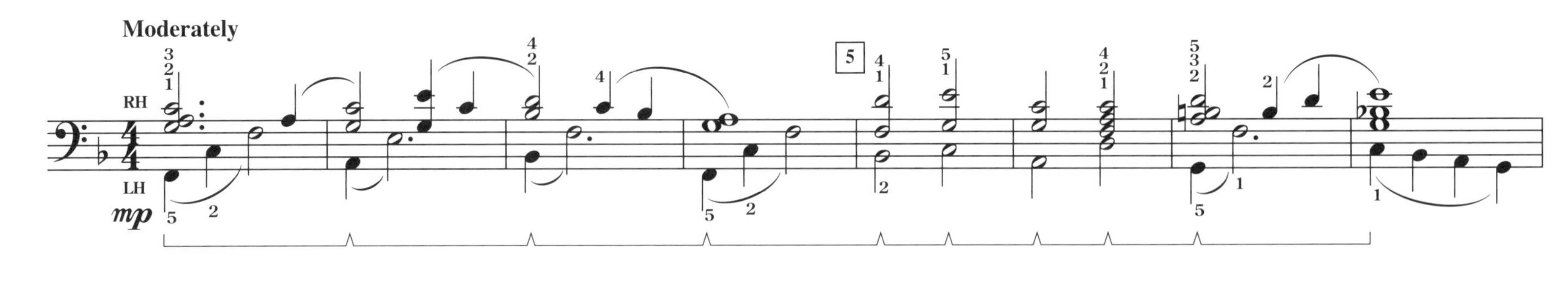

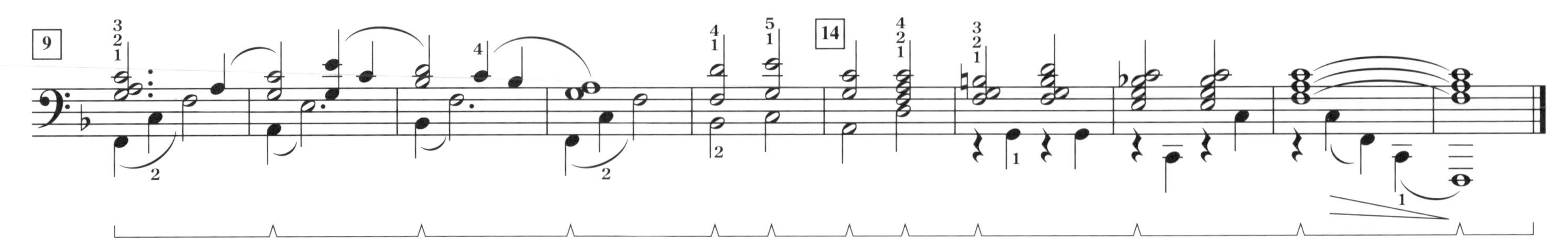

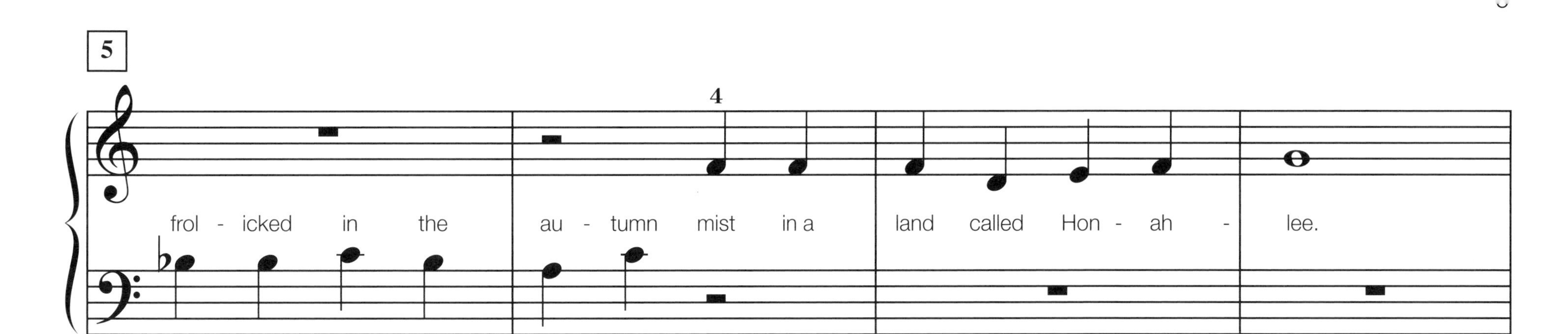
5
4
frol - icked in the
au - tumn mist in a
land called Hon - ah - lee.
2

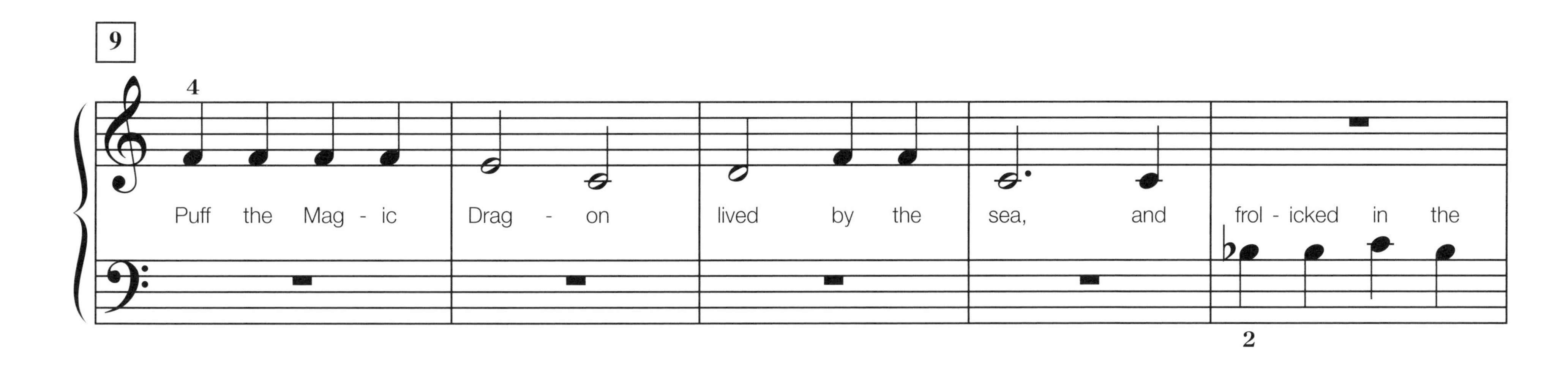
9
4
Puff the Mag - ic
Drag - on
lived by the
sea, and
frol - icked in the
2

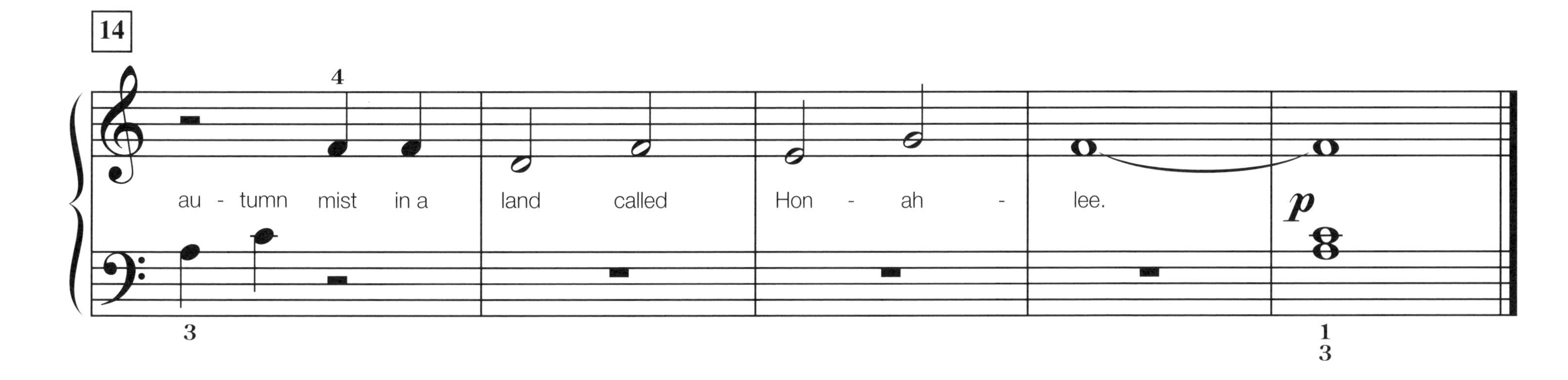
14
4
au - tumn mist in a
land called
Hon - ah -
lee.
p
3
1
3

This Land Is Your Land

Words and Music by Woody Guthrie
Arranged by Carol Matz

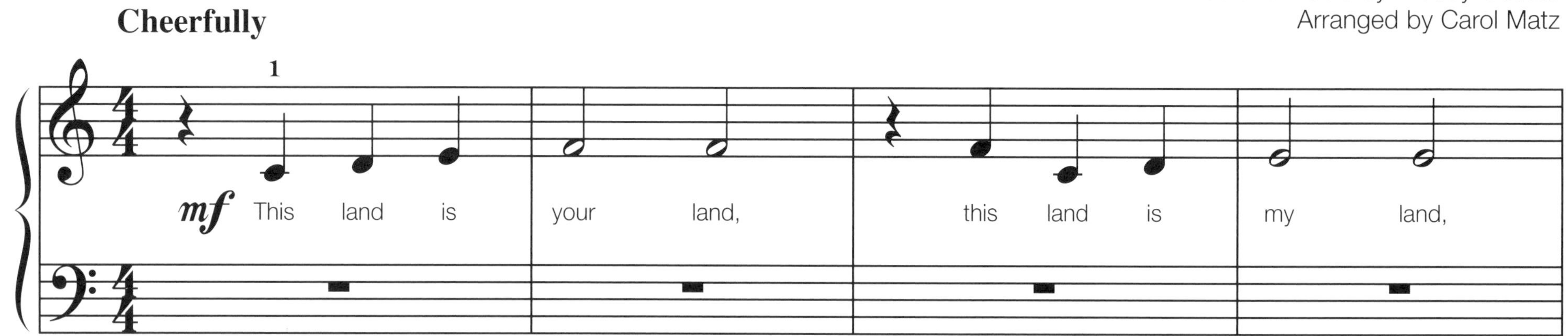

DUET PART (Student plays one octave higher)

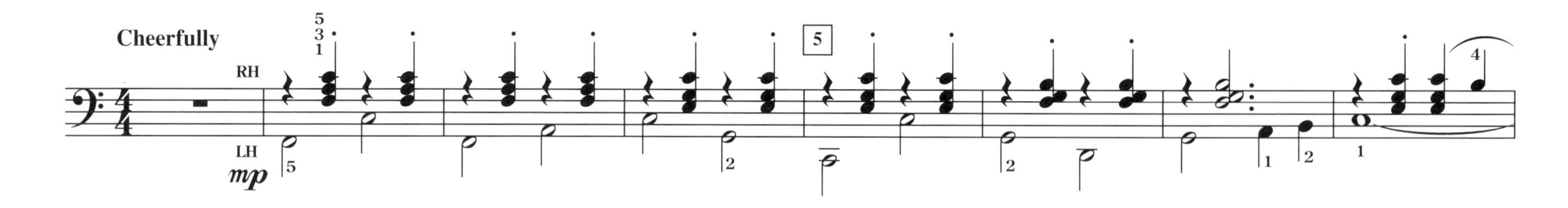

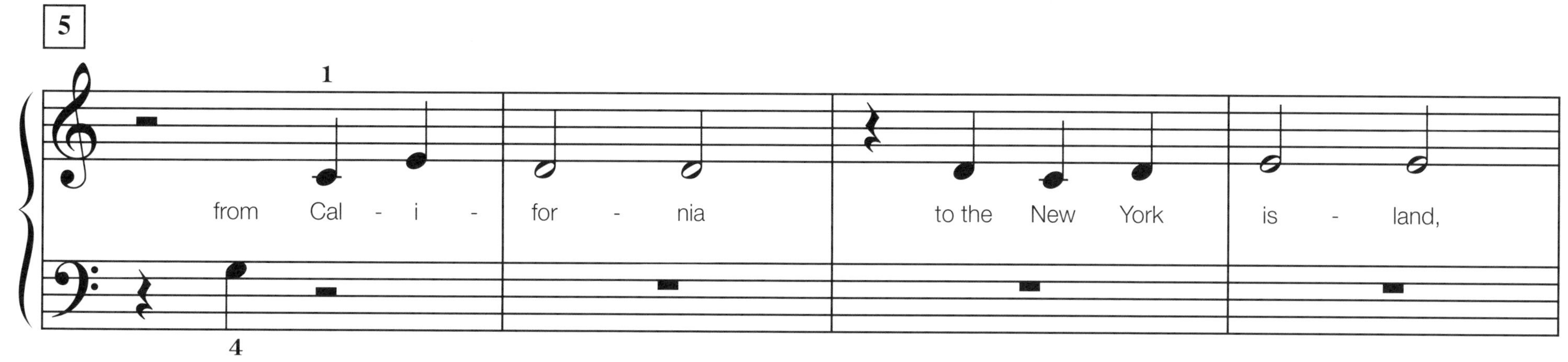
5
1
from Cal - i - for - nia to the New York is - land,
4

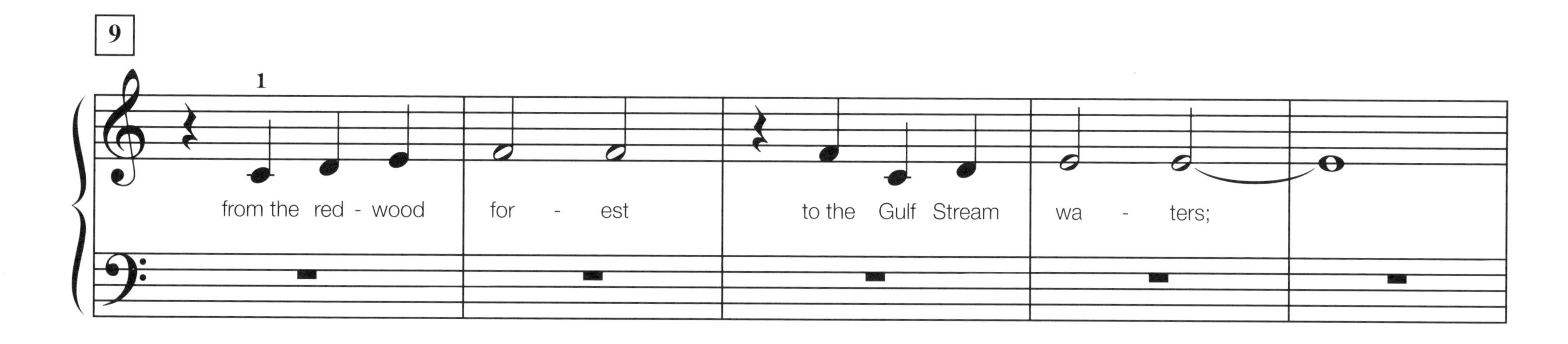
9
1
from the red - wood for - est to the Gulf Stream wa - ters;

14
this land was made for you and me.
2

Peter Cottontail

Words and Music by
Steve Nelson and Jack Rollins
Arranged by Carol Matz

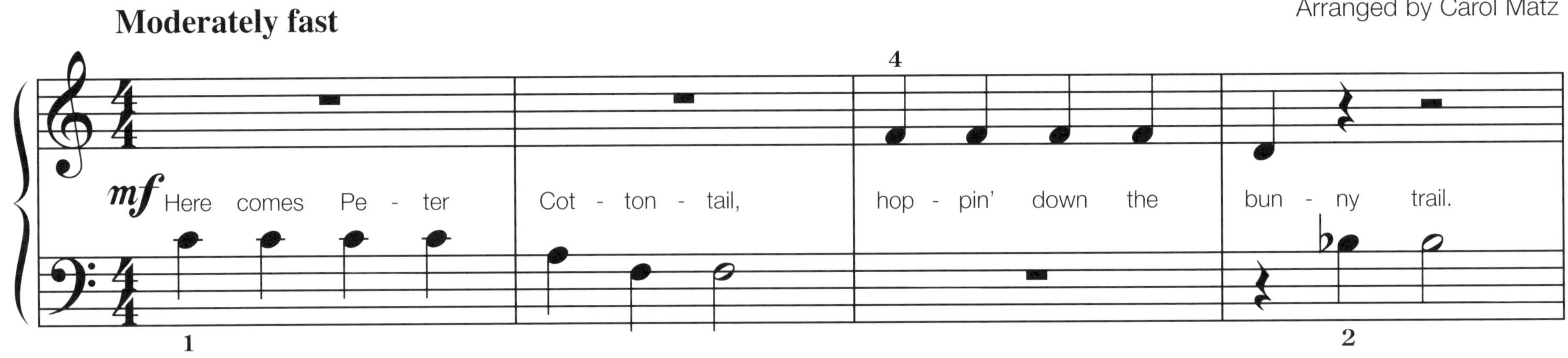

DUET PART (Student plays one octave higher)

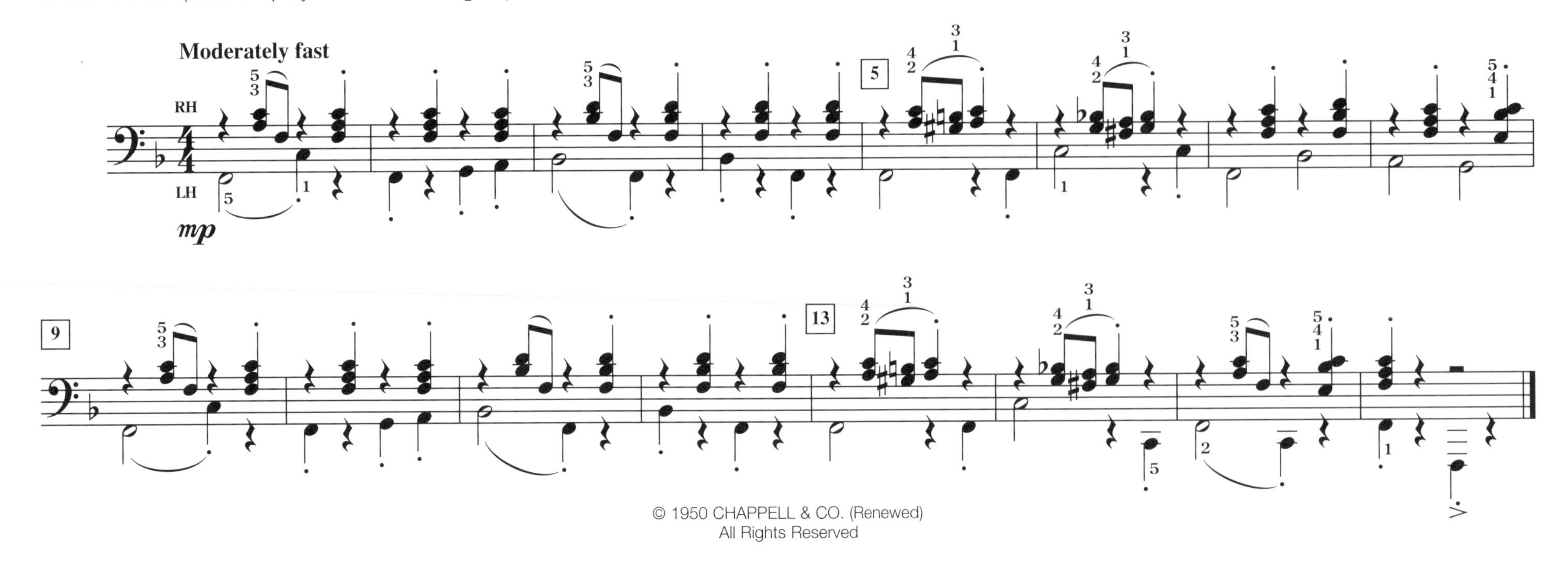

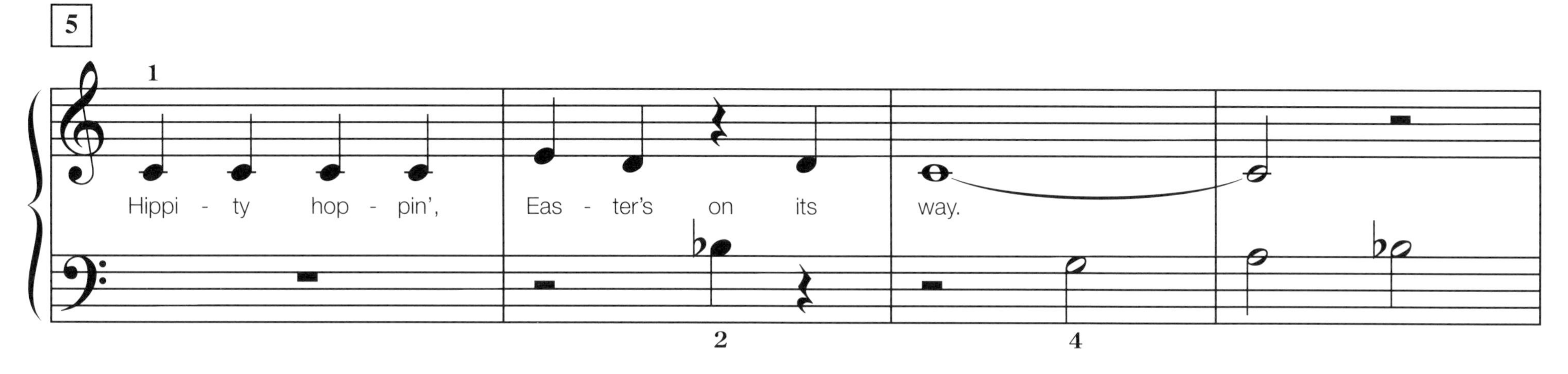
5
1
Hippi - ty hop - pin',
Eas - ter's on its
way.
2
4

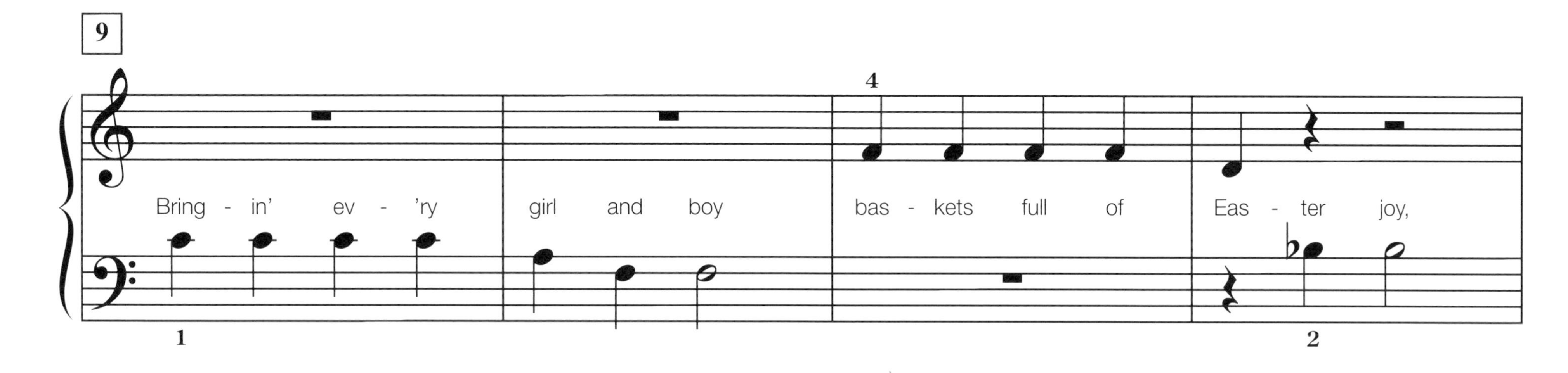
9
4
Bring - in' ev - 'ry
girl and boy
bas - kets full of
Eas - ter joy,
1
2

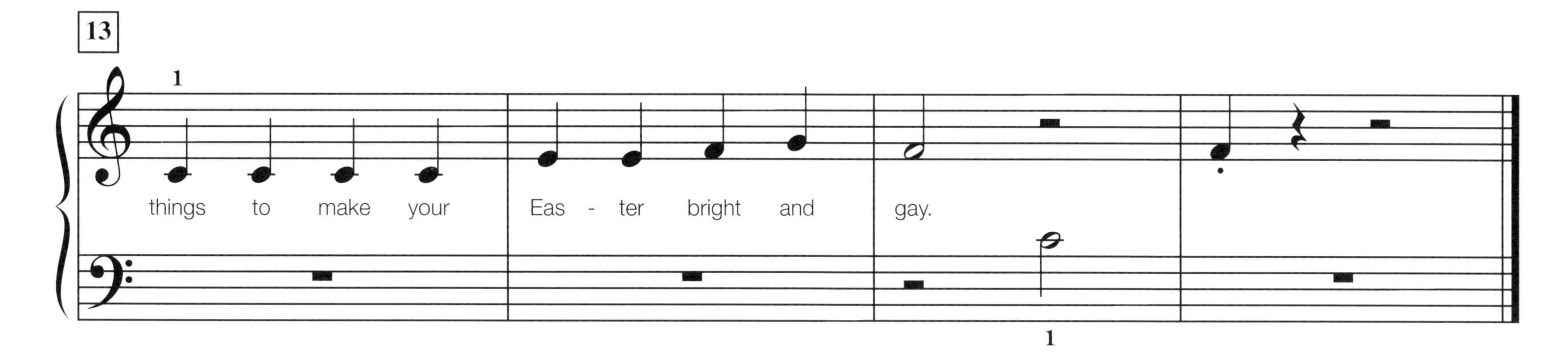
13
1
things to make your
Eas - ter bright and
gay.
1

Scooby Doo, Where Are You?

Words and Music by
David Mook and Ben Raleigh
Arranged by Carol Matz

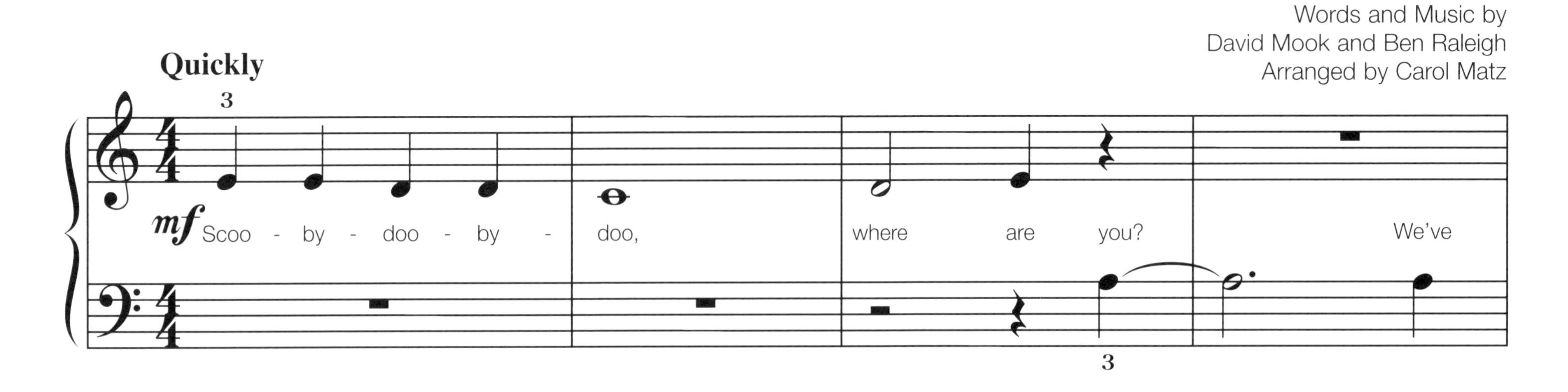

DUET PART (Student plays one octave higher)

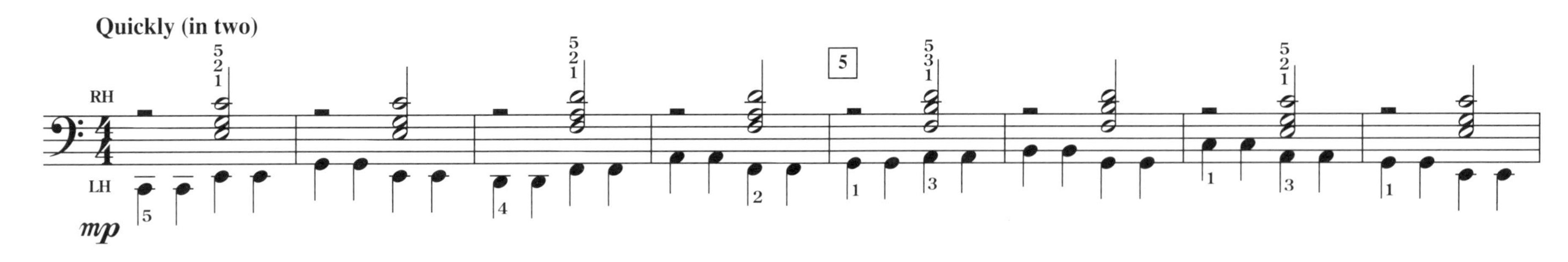

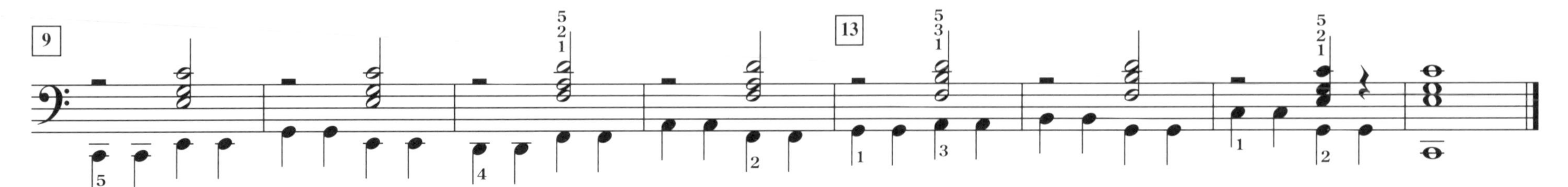

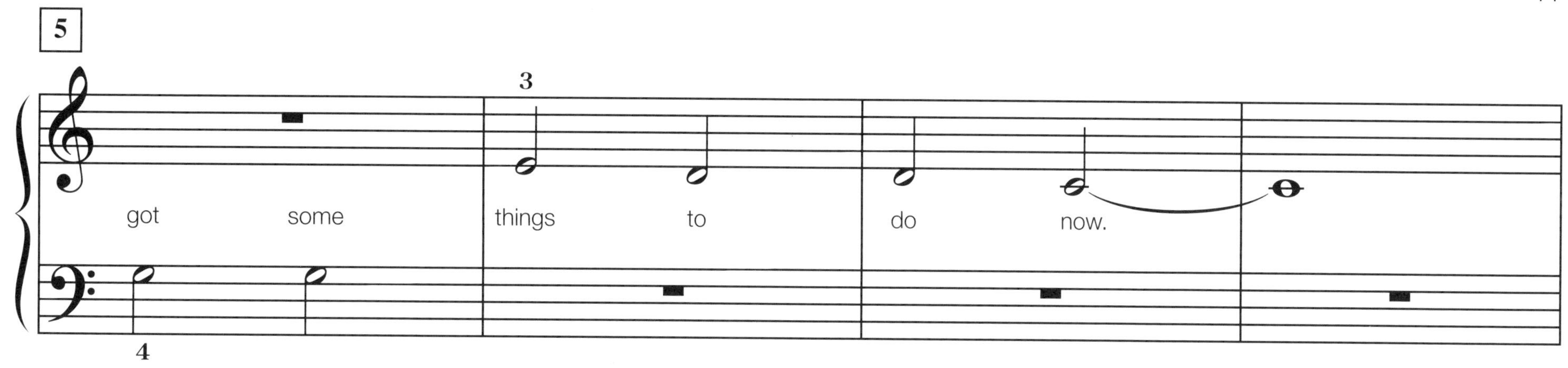
5
3
got
some
things
to
do
now.
4

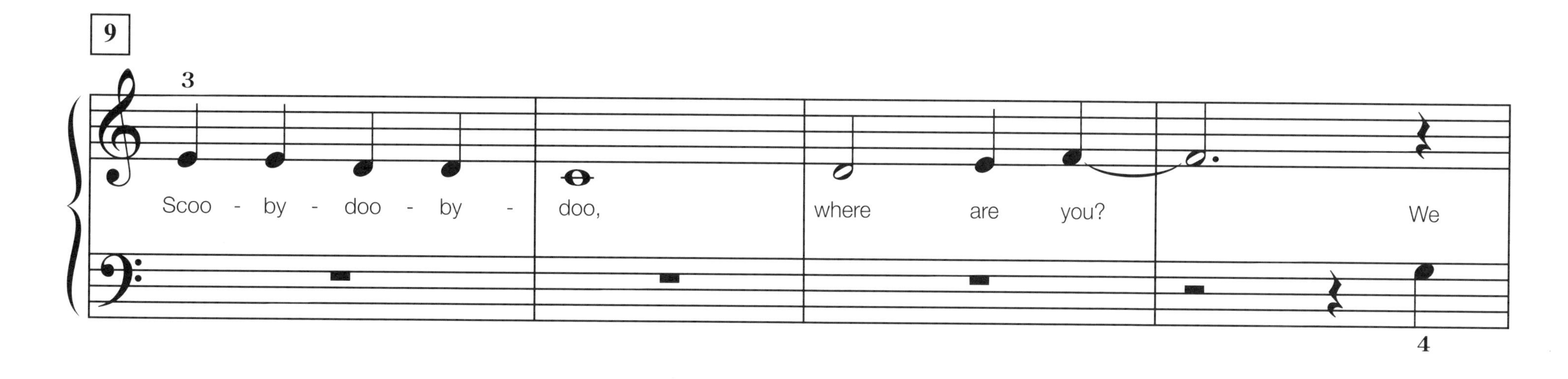
9
3
Scoo - by - doo - by - doo,
where
are
you?
We
4

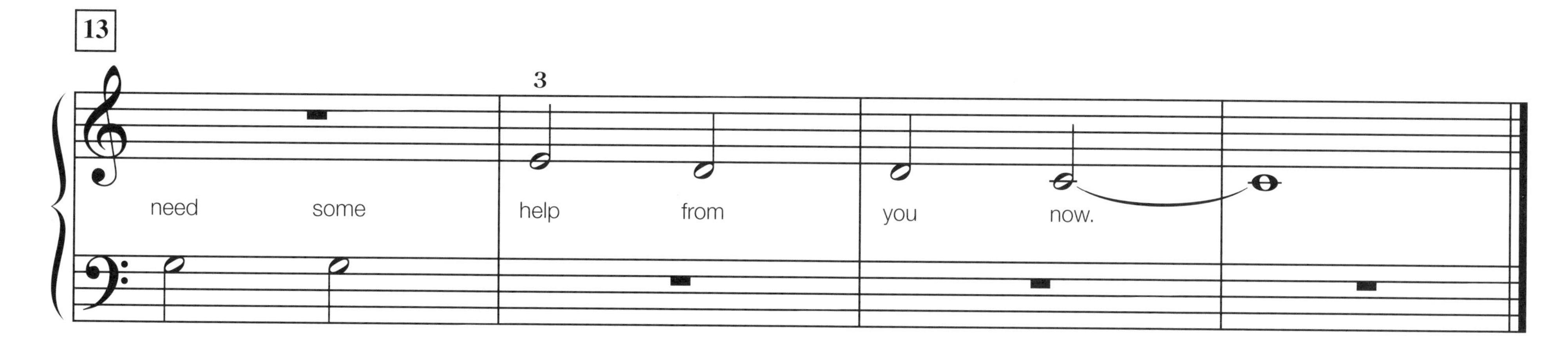
13
3
need
some
help
from
you
now.

This Is It!

(Theme from "The Bugs Bunny Show")

Words and Music by
Mack David and Jerry Livingston
Arranged by Carol Matz

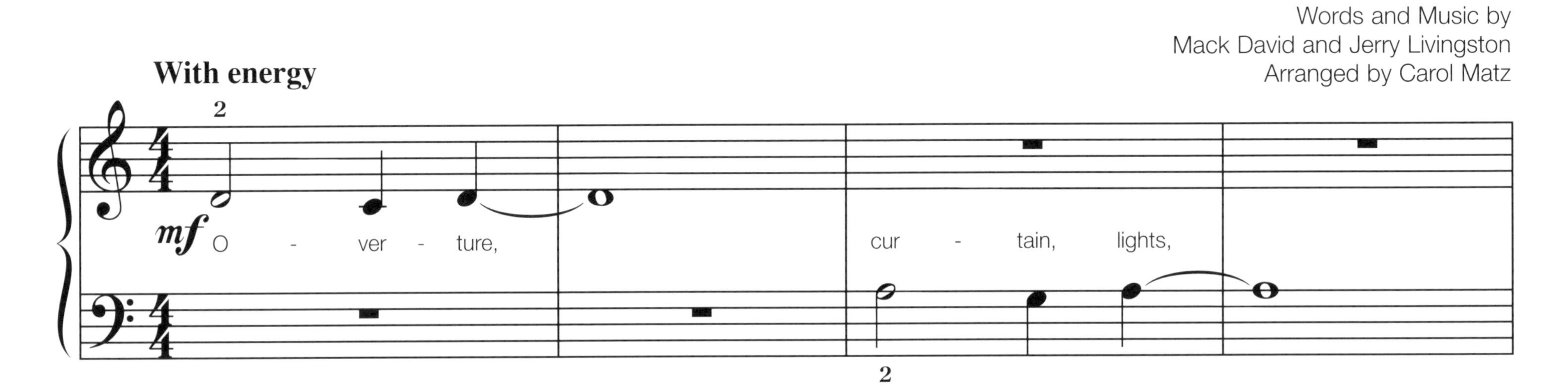

DUET PART (Student plays one octave higher)

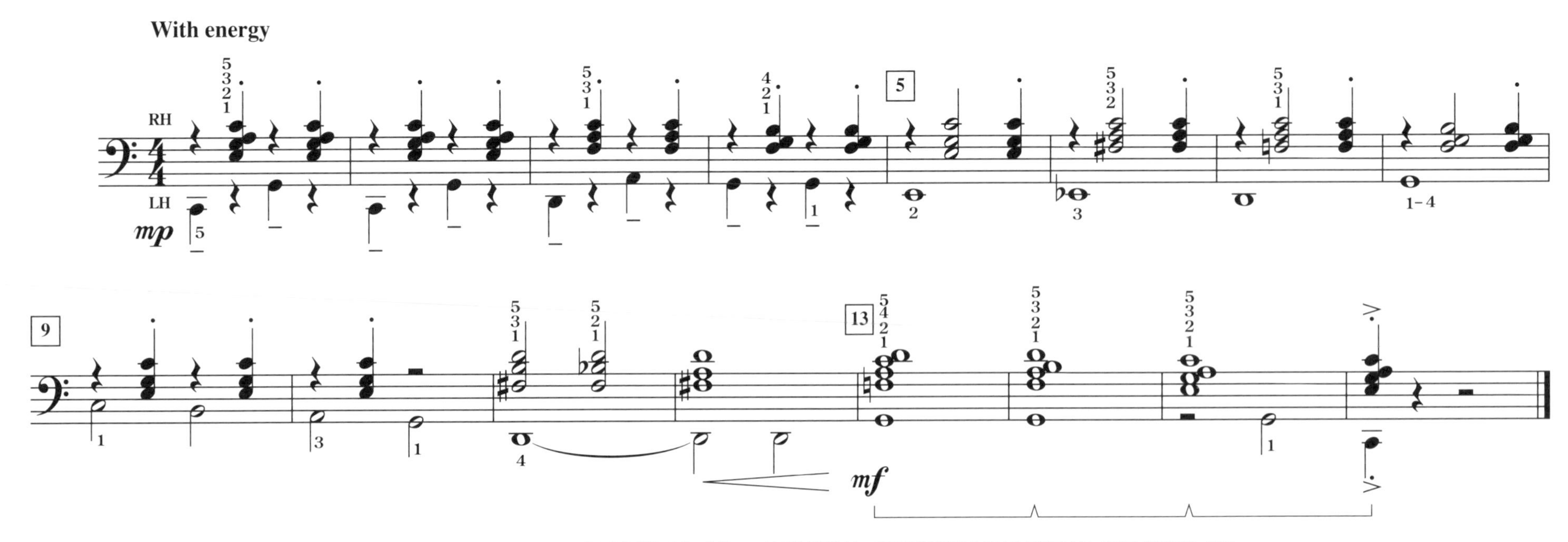

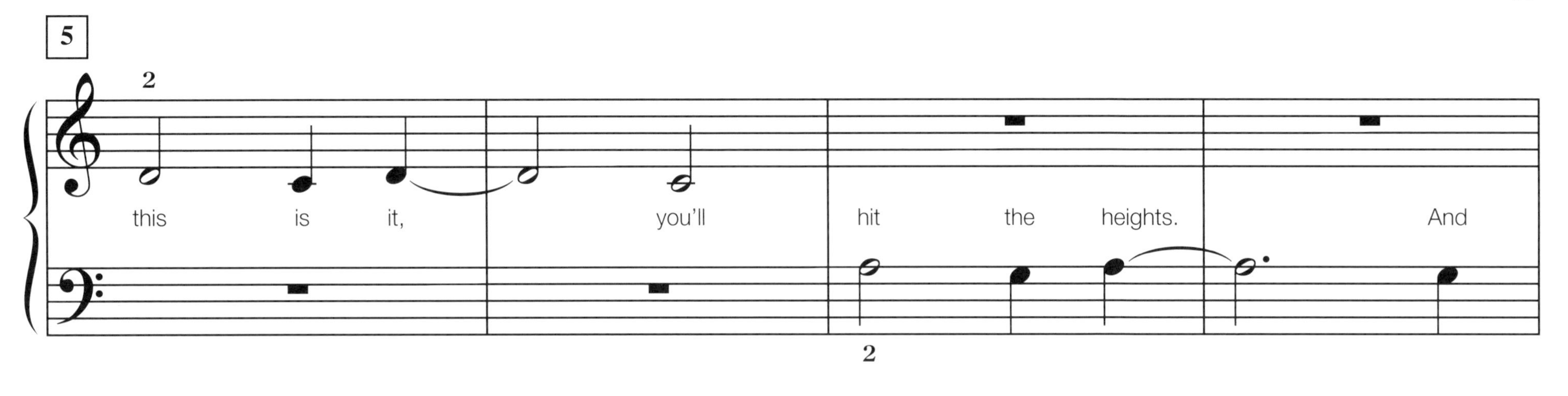
5
2
this is it, you'll
hit the heights. And
2

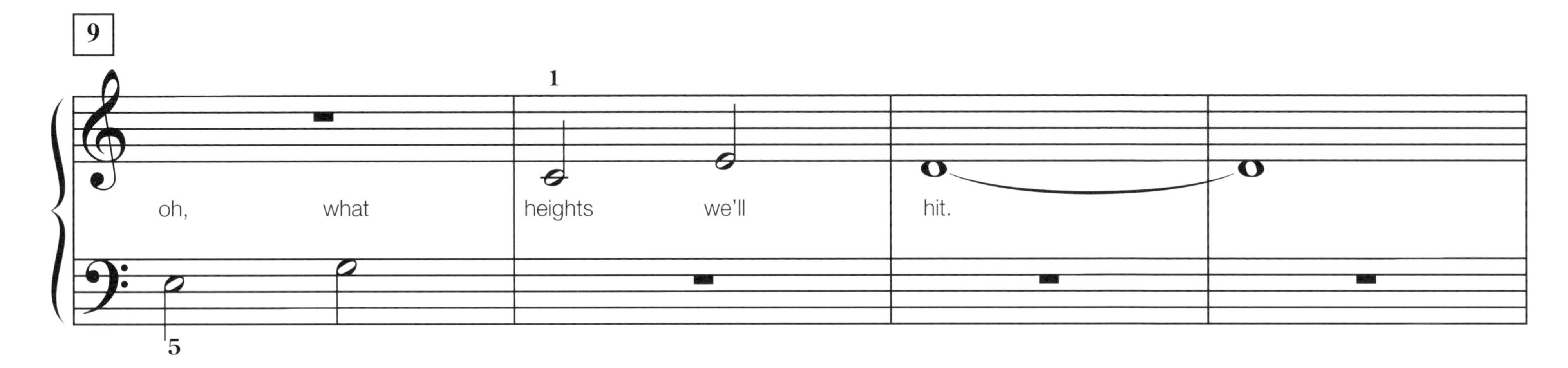
9
1
oh, what heights we'll hit.
5

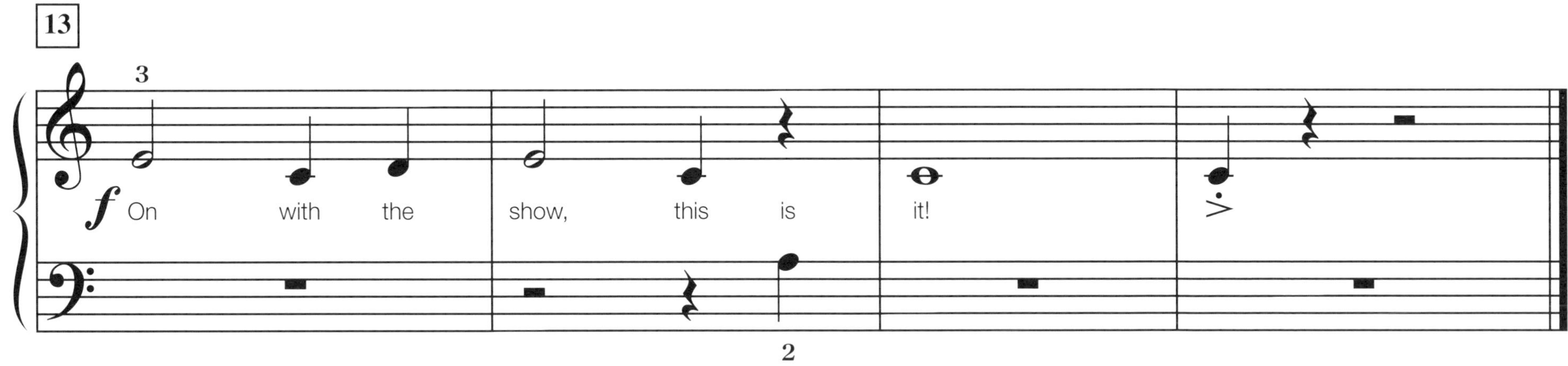
13
3
f On with the show, this is it!
2

The Merry-Go-Round Broke Down

Words and Music by
Cliff Friend and Dave Franklin
Arranged by Carol Matz

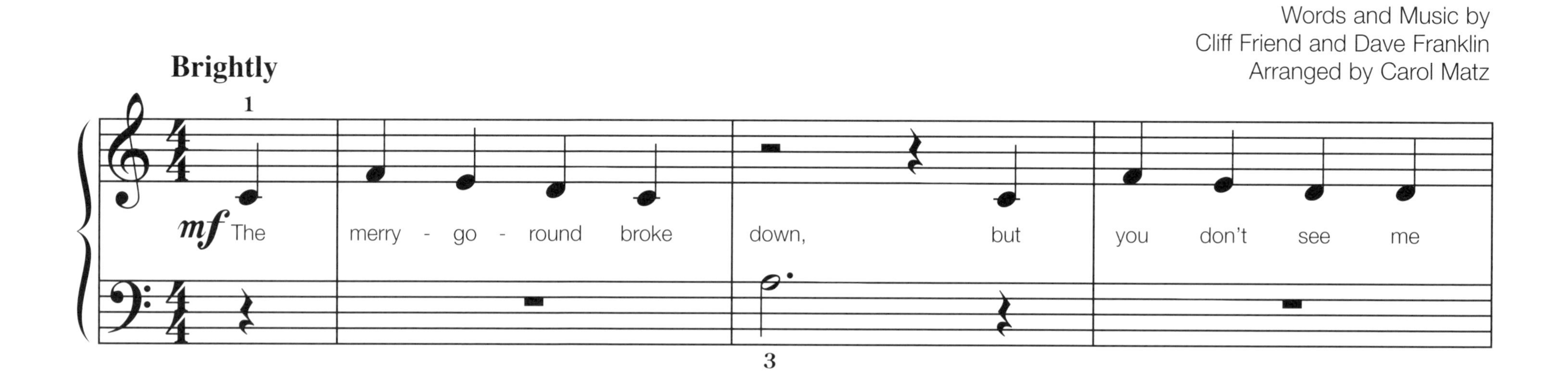

DUET PART (Student plays one octave higher)

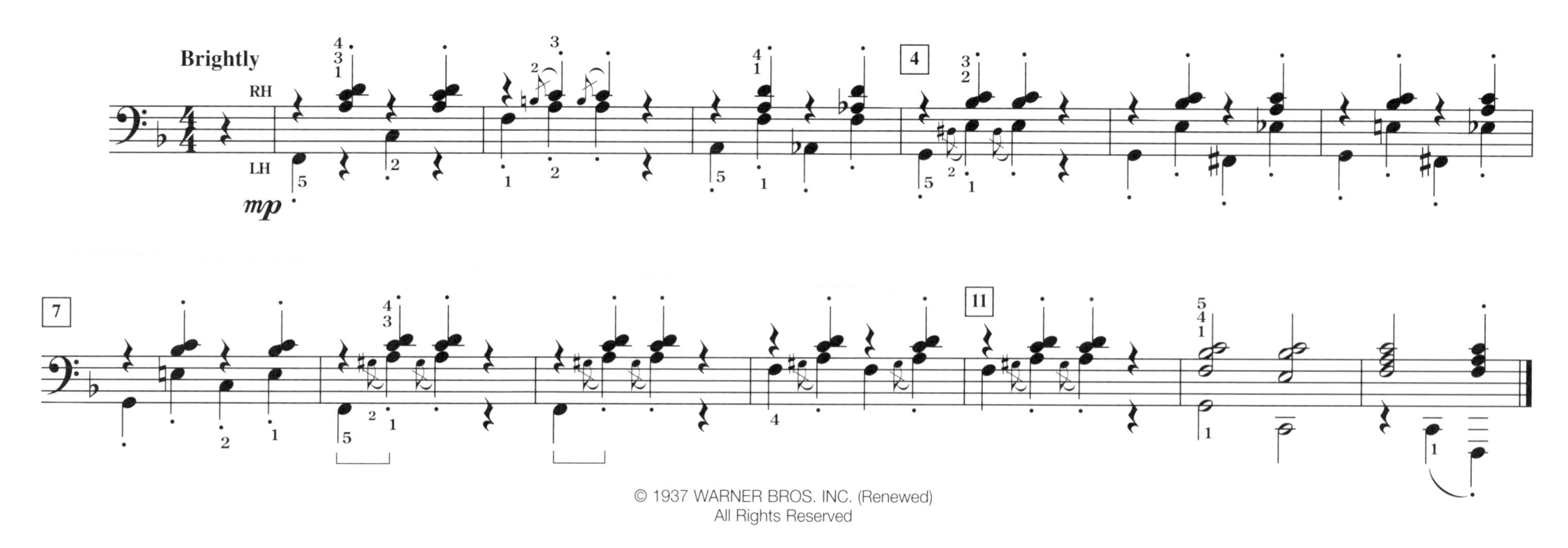

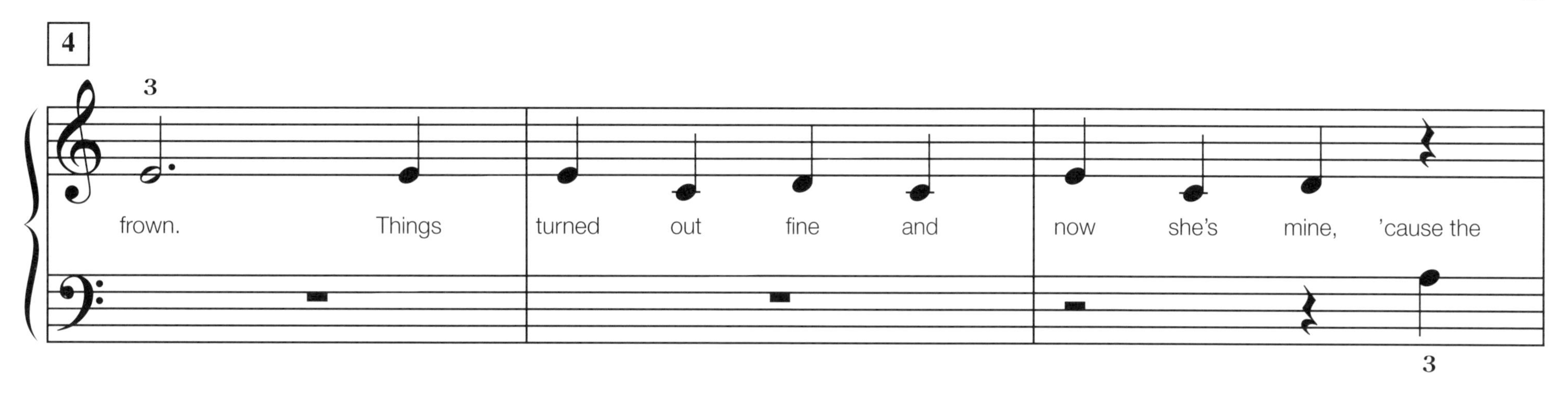
4
3
frown. Things turned out fine and now she's mine, 'cause the
3

7
4
merry - go - round went oom - pah - pah, oom - pah - pah, oom - pah, oom - pah,
4 2 5

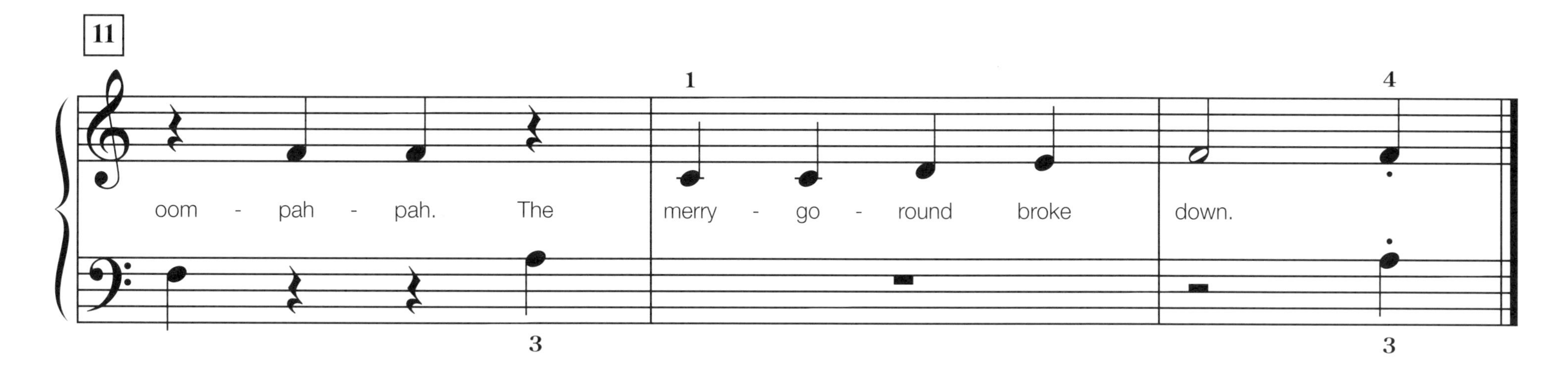
11
1 4
oom - pah - pah. The merry - go - round broke down.
3 3

The Ballad of Gilligan's Isle

Words and Music by
Sherwood Schwartz and George Wyle
Arranged by Carol Matz

DUET PART (Student plays one octave higher)

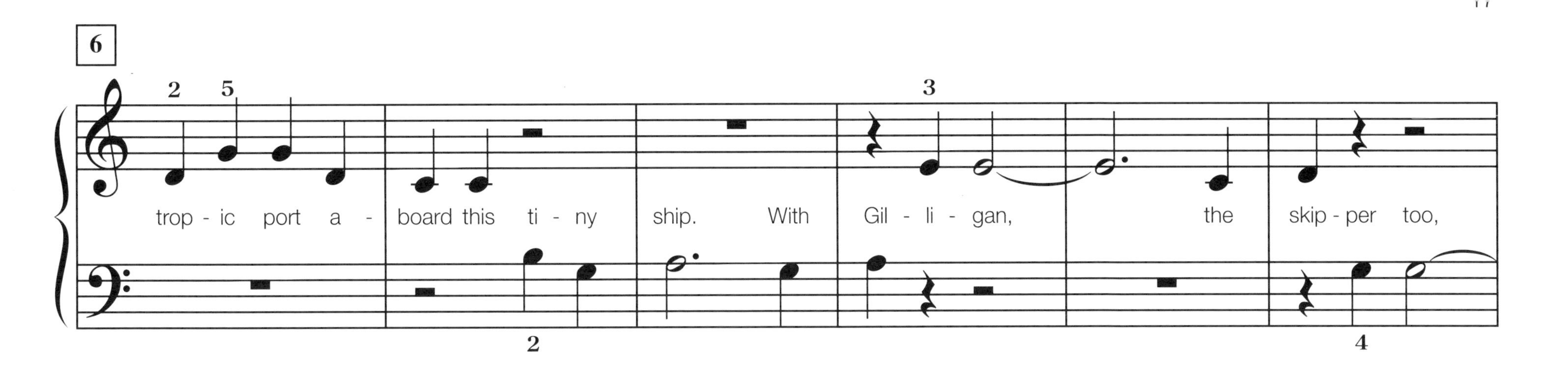
6
2 5
3
trop - ic port a - board this ti - ny ship. With Gil - li - gan, the skip - per too,
2
4

12
3
the mil - lion - aire and his wife. The mov - ie star,
2

18
3
1
the pro - fes - sor and Mar - y Ann, f here on Gil - li - gan's Isle!
3

Over the Rainbow

(from the M-G-M Motion Picture "The Wizard of Oz")

Music by Harold Arlen
Lyric by E. Y. Harburg
Arranged by Carol Matz

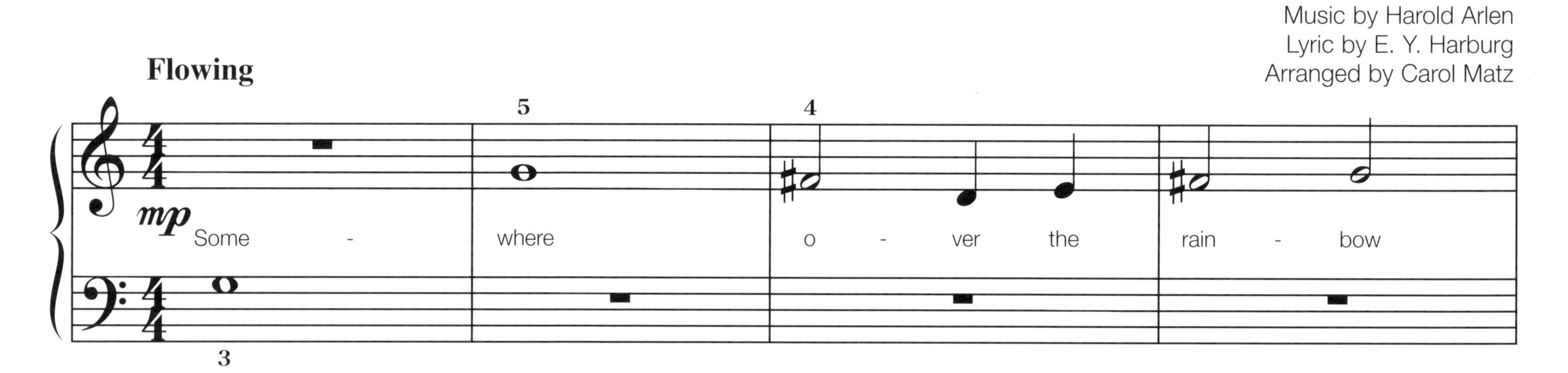

DUET PART (Student plays one octave higher)

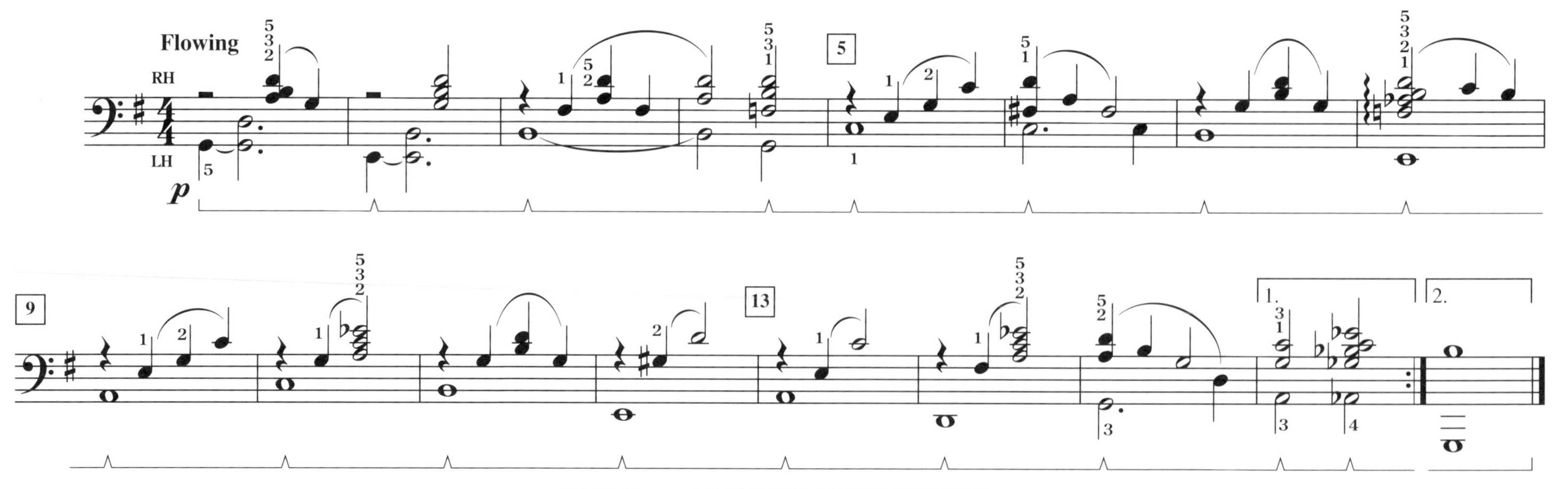

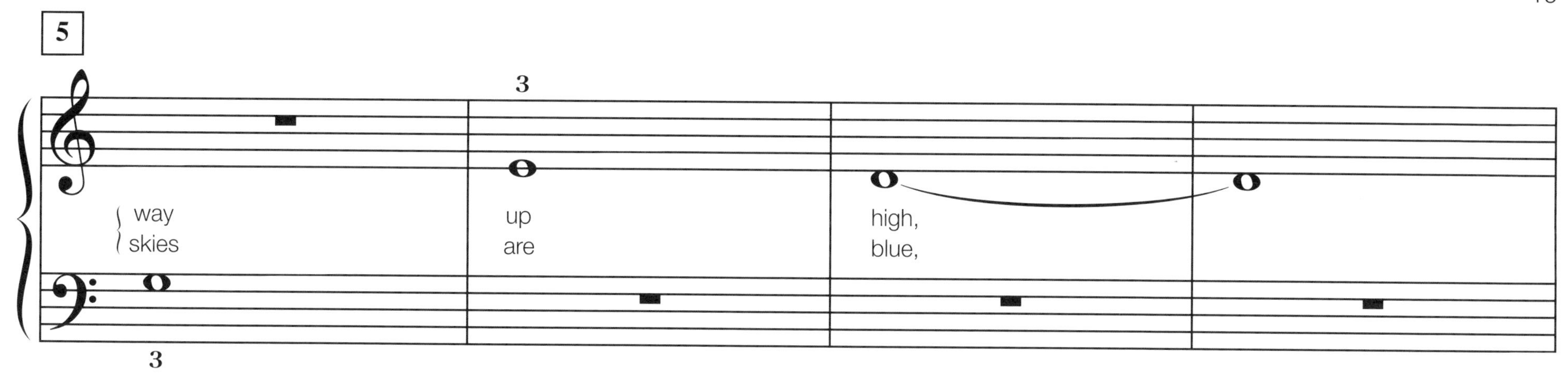
5
3
way
skies
up
are
high,
blue,
3

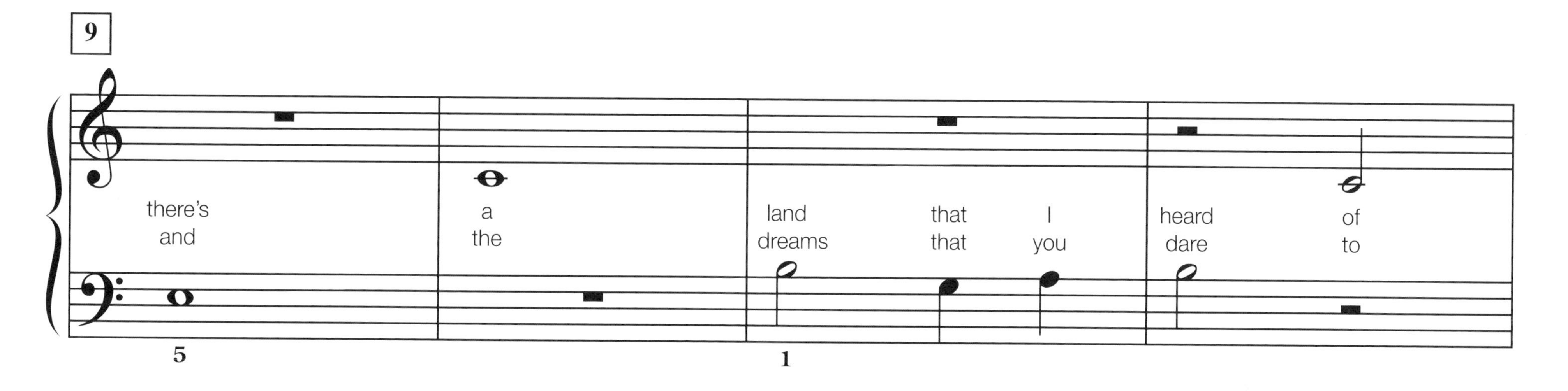
9
there's
and
a
the
land
dreams
that
that
I
you
heard
dare
of
to
5
1

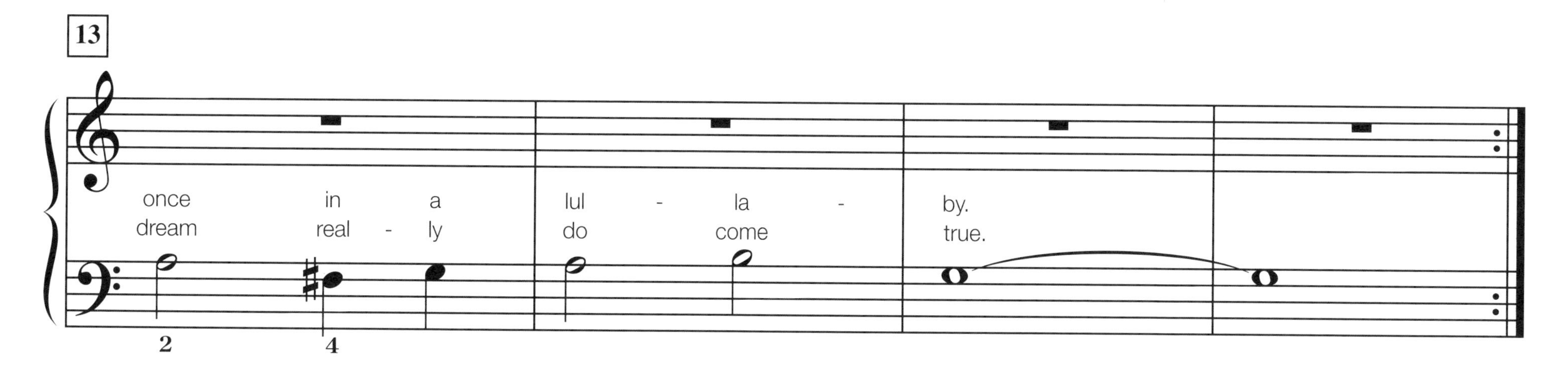
13
once
dream
in
real - ly
a
lul - la -
do
come
by.
true.
2
4

Theme from Inspector Gadget

Words and Music by
Haim Saban and Shuki Levy
Arranged by Carol Matz

DUET PART (Student plays one octave higher)

5
1
5
4
3
9
1
2
1
3

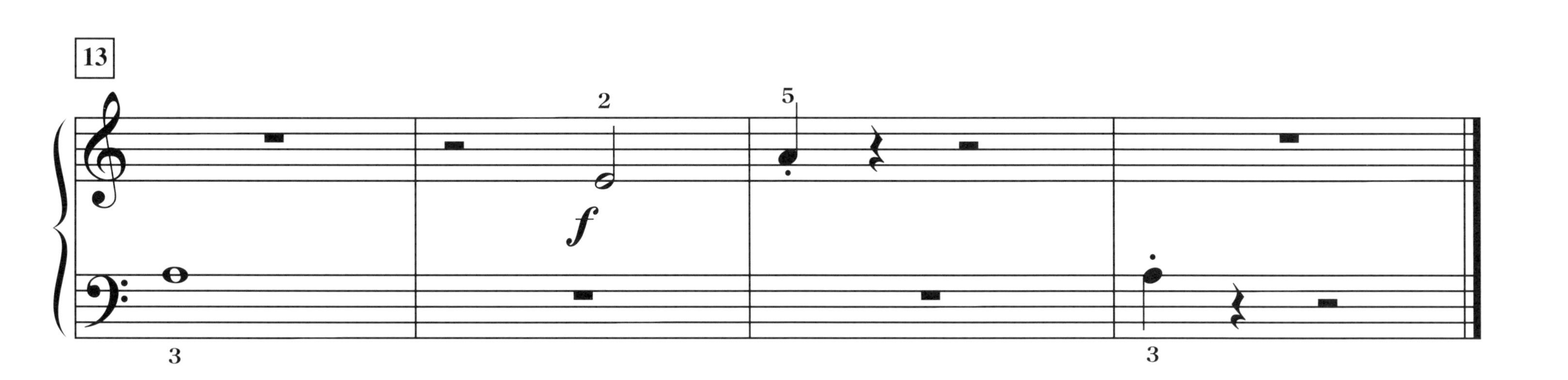
13
2
5
f
3
3

Can You Feel the Love Tonight

(from Walt Disney's "The Lion King")

Music by Elton John
Words by Tim Rice
Arranged by Carol Matz

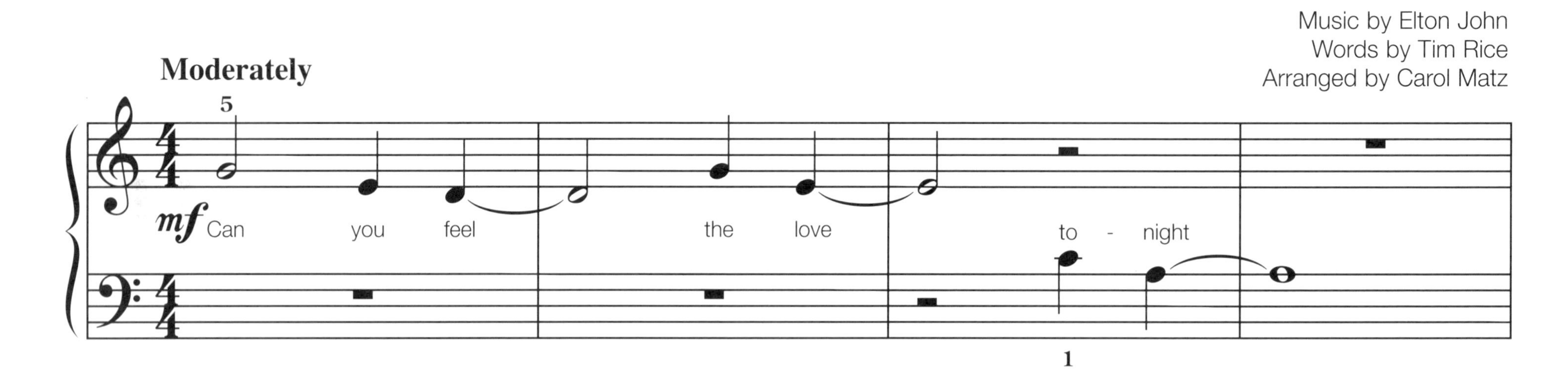

DUET PART (Student plays one octave higher)

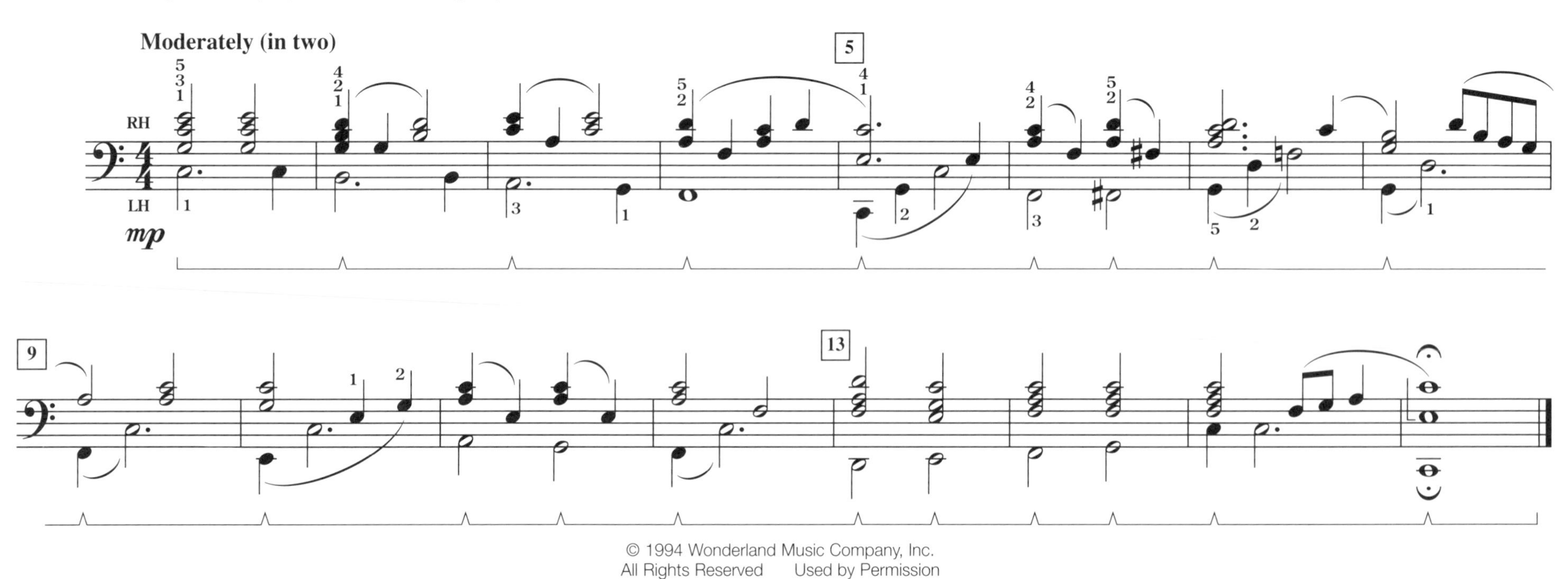

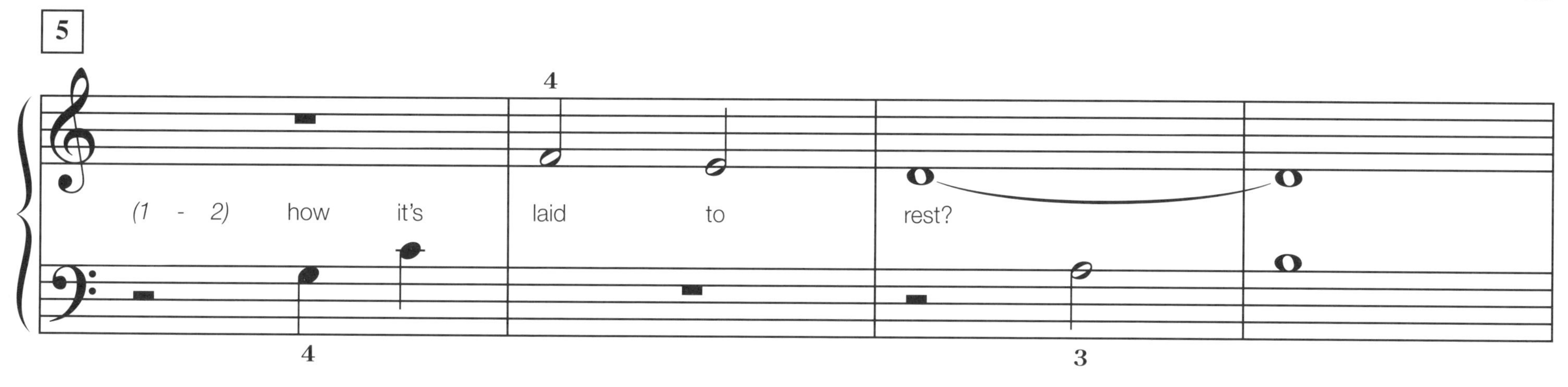
5
4
(1 - 2) how it's
laid to
rest?
4
3

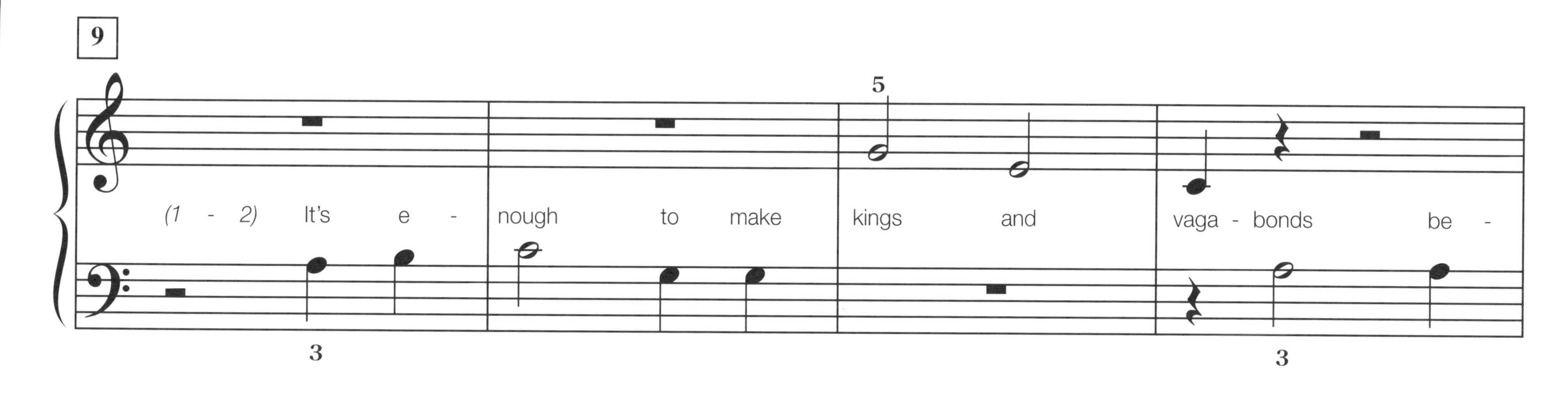
9
5
(1 - 2) It's e -
nough to make
kings and
vaga - bonds be -
3
3

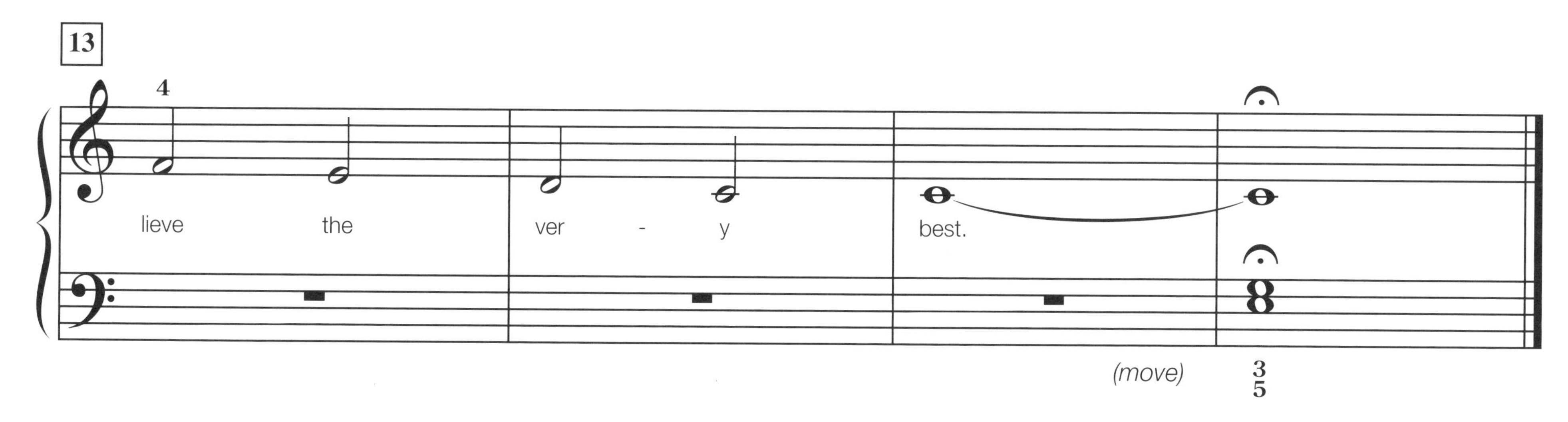
13
4
lieve the
ver - y
best.
(move)
3
5

Alfred